... To your heart's content !

Happy Birthday

to the Best Friend in the world.

(I expect to be sampling some of this pretty soon!)

love from Janetta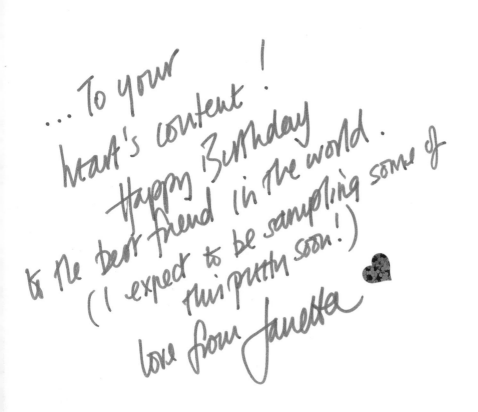

CHOCOLATE
BAKING

CHOCOLATE
BAKING

LINDA COLLISTER
Photography by
Patrice de Villiers

RYLAND
PETERS
& SMALL

Art Director **Jacqui Small**

Art Editor **Penny Stock**

Editor **Elsa Petersen-Schepelern**

Photography **Patrice de Villiers**

Food Stylist **Linda Collister**

Stylist **Penny Markham**

Production **Kate Mackillop**

For Emily

Notes: Ovens should be preheated to the specified temperature – if using a fan-assisted oven, adjust time and temperature according to the manufacturer's instructions.

First Published in Great Britain in 1997
by Ryland Peters & Small
Cavendish House, 51-55 Mortimer Street, London W1N 7TD

Text © Linda Collister 1997
Design and photographs © Ryland Peters & Small 1996
Reprinted in 1998

Printed and bound in Hong Kong

ISBN 1 900518 38 4

A CIP record for this book is available from the British Library

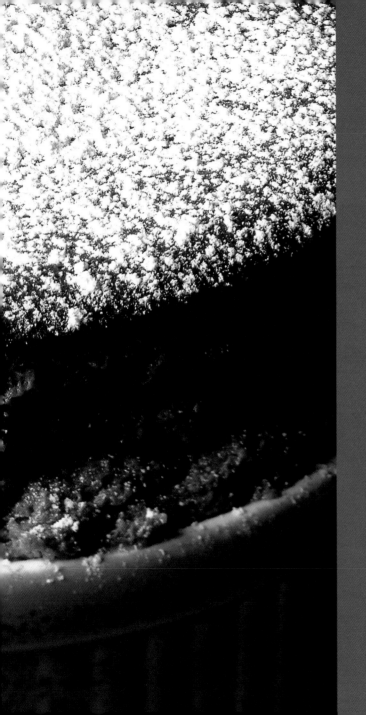

CONTENTS

chocolate
baking

Eating chocolate is **pure joy**, cooking with it a delight, even smelling it bewitching, but buying it shakes my faith in human nature.

The best chocolate is wonderful, but most is not worth buying and most people buy terrible stuff. Good quality plain or dark chocolate will taste **smooth** not greasy, **bitter** not raw, **intense** not oversweet, with a **long finish,** not a cloying aftertaste.

But how do you know good quality? Price is not a reliable guide – in fact supermarkets' **own brands** are usually excellent and are a good bargain when buying in bulk for cooking.

The quality and taste of chocolate is determined by the quantity and quality of the **cocoa solids** – the dry solids plus the added cocoa butter – used in its production. The quantity of solids, at least, is indicated on the packet. **Couverture** chocolate, used for fillings and icings, usually has around 55 per cent cocoa solids; **bitter** chocolate around 65 per cent; and **super amer** or **extra bitter**, best for puddings, fine cakes and eating, is just over 70 per cent. Some chocolates labelled 'for cooking' can contain as little as 30 per cent cocoa solids: the rest is sugar, fats and flavourings.

The raw material for chocolate is the cocoa bean, found in the large yellow-green fruits of the *Theobroma cacao* tree which grows only within 20 degrees north or south of the equator. Each tree yields enough beans to make around 2.5 kg of chocolate each year. The best chocolate is made from a **blend of beans** – each type has its own individual character and colour ranging from pale coffee through to dark mahogany brown.

Store chocolate well away from other foods in an airtight container in a **cool, dry place,** because it can easily be tainted by other flavours. Avoid storing chocolate below 13°C, or in the fridge, as beads of moisture will form when you bring it to room temperature.

Don't store in a hot kitchen (30°C or above) or it will develop a white bloom as the cocoa butter comes to the surface. The bloom does not affect its taste however – it can still used for cooking. Chocolate begins melting at 30°C (that's why it melts in the mouth) and burns at 110°C. Melt it **slowly and gradually** as it easily becomes overheated and scorched, and turns into an unusable solid mass. Chop it into evenly sized pieces so it melts at the same rate. Place in a shallow, heatproof bowl set over a pan of steaming hot, not boiling, water. The water must not touch the base of the bowl, and no drop of water or steam should touch the chocolate or it will seize up. Stir **frequently**, and remove from the heat as soon as it melts.

almond
chocolate kugelhopf

400 g strong white bread flour

½ teaspoon sea salt

15 g fresh yeast

60 g golden caster sugar

200 ml skimmed milk, lukewarm

3 medium eggs, beaten

100 g unsalted butter, softened

50 g slivered or flaked almonds

60 g plain chocolate,
roughly chopped

Nut Coating:

25 g unsalted butter, very soft

50 g slivered or flaked almonds

icing sugar, for dusting

one 23 cm kugelhopf mould

Makes 1 large cake

*To use easy-blend dried yeast,
mix one 7 g sachet with 140 g of
the flour. Mix in the sugar and milk
and let rise for 30 minutes. Make a
well in the remaining flour, add the
salt, add the yeast liquid and eggs
and proceed with the recipe.*

To make the nut coating, thickly butter the inside of the
kugelhopf mould with the very soft butter, then press the
almonds all around. Chill while preparing the dough.

To make the dough, mix the flour and salt in a large mixing
bowl, then make a well in the centre.

Crumble the yeast into a small bowl, then cream to a smooth
liquid with the sugar and milk. Pour into the well, and work in
enough flour to make a thick batter.

Cover with a damp tea towel, and leave at normal room
temperature for 30 minutes. The batter should look bubbly.

Add the eggs to the yeast liquid, stir until combined, then
gradually beat in the flour to make a soft and very sticky
dough. Beat the dough in the bowl with your hand or with the
dough hook in an electric mixer for about 5 minutes or until it
becomes firmer, smooth, very elastic and shiny.

Work in the soft butter until thoroughly incorporated, then the
almonds and chocolate. When evenly mixed, carefully spoon
the soft dough into the prepared mould (it should be half full).
Cover the mould with a damp tea towel and let rise at normal
room temperature until the dough has almost doubled in size
and has risen to about 2.5 cm below the rim of the mould –
about 1 hour.

Bake in a preheated oven at 200°C (400°F) Gas 6 for about
45 minutes, or until the cake is golden brown and a skewer
inserted into the dough midway between the outer edge and
inner tube comes out clean. Leave to cool for 1 minute, then

carefully unmould on to a wire rack and let cool completely.
Serve dusted with icing sugar.
Store in an airtight container and eat with 3 days or freeze for
up to 1 month. It can also be lightly toasted under a grill.

Variations:

Marbled Kugelhopf

Replace 50 g of the strong white bread flour with 50 g sieved
cocoa powder and 25 g sugar. Replace the 60 g plain
chocolate with a similar quantity of white chocolate, roughly
chopped. Proceed as in the main recipe.

Sultana Kugelhopf

Replace 50 g of the strong white bread flour with 50 g sieved
cocoa powder and 25 g sugar. Replace the 60 g plain
chocolate with a similar quantity of sultanas or raisins.
Proceed as in the main recipe.

*Note: both cocoa variations of this recipe are delicious
toasted and spread with peanut butter.*

This **pretty,** yeast coffee-time cake is made in a traditional earthenware mould, a tube pan or non-stick ring mould. Serve it either **plain** or toasted.

*A **great** combination of bitter chocolate and ginger in syrup.*

chocolate gingerbread

150 g dark chocolate, chopped

150 g unsalted butter,
at room temperature

150 g golden caster sugar

3 large eggs, separated

50 g ground almonds

120 g self-raising flour

1 tablespoon cocoa powder

3 pieces stem ginger, chopped

2 tablespoons syrup
from jar of stem ginger

Chocolate Topping:

40 g dark chocolate, chopped

15 g unsalted butter

1 tablespoon syrup
from jar of stem ginger

1 piece of stem ginger, sliced,
to finish

one 22 x 11 x 7 cm loaf tin,
greased and base-lined

Makes 1 cake

Very gently melt the chocolate in a heatproof bowl set over a pan of steaming water. Stir until smooth, remove from the heat and let cool. Using an electric mixer or wooden spoon, beat the butter until creamy, then gradually beat in the sugar. Beat until light and fluffy, then beat in the egg yolks one at a time, beating well after each addition.

Beat in the cooled chocolate, then sift the almonds, flour and cocoa into the bowl. Add the chopped ginger and syrup, and fold in using a large metal spoon.

Whisk the egg whites until stiff peaks form, then fold into the mixture in 3 batches.

Spoon the mixture into the prepared tin and smooth the surface. Bake in a preheated oven at 190°C (375°F) Gas 5 for about 40 minutes or until a skewer inserted into the centre of the cake comes out clean. Leave for 5 minutes, then turn out on to a wire rack and let cool completely.

To make the topping, melt the chocolate, butter and syrup in a heatproof bowl set over a pan of steaming water. Stir until smooth, then spoon over the top of the cake. When almost set, decorate with finely sliced, diced or grated stem ginger. Store in an airtight container and eat within 1 week – it improves in taste after several days. If undecorated, it can be frozen for up to 1 month.

marbled fudge cake

80 g digestive biscuits, crushed

50 g unsalted butter, melted

Chocolate Mixture:

120 g plain chocolate, chopped

35 g unsalted butter, diced,
at room temperature

2 large eggs

150 g golden caster sugar

75 g plain flour

a pinch of salt

½ teaspoon baking powder

2–3 drops real vanilla essence

50 g walnut pieces or pecans

Vanilla Mixture:

25 g unsalted butter

½ teaspoon real vanilla essence

85 g Philadelphia cream cheese

50 g golden caster sugar

1 large egg, beaten

10 g plain flour

one 21 cm springform pan, greased

Makes 1 cake (16 slices)

To make the base, mix the biscuit crumbs with the melted butter, then press into the base of the tin to make a thin, even layer. Chill while preparing the filling.

To make the chocolate mixture, melt the chocolate gently in a heatproof bowl set over a pan of barely simmering water. Stir until smooth, remove from the heat and stir in the butter.

In another bowl beat the eggs and sugar with a wooden spoon until frothy. Sift the flour, salt and baking powder into the bowl and stir well. Add the mixed melted chocolate and butter and the vanilla. Chop the nuts, add to the bowl and mix well. Spread the mixture over the base.

To make the vanilla mixture, bring the butter to room temperature, then beat until creamy using a wooden spoon or electric mixer. Beat in the vanilla and cream cheese until the mixture is light and fluffy. Gradually beat in the sugar, then the egg. Add the flour and stir well.

Spoon the mixture on top of the chocolate and swirl the tip of a knife through the mixtures giving a marbled effect.

Bake in a preheated oven at 180°C (350°F) Gas 4 for about 25 minutes until just firm. Let cool in the tin before unmoulding. Serve at room temperature.

Store in an airtight container and eat within 5 days, or freeze for up to 1 month.

This cake *improves* in flavour for *several days* after baking.

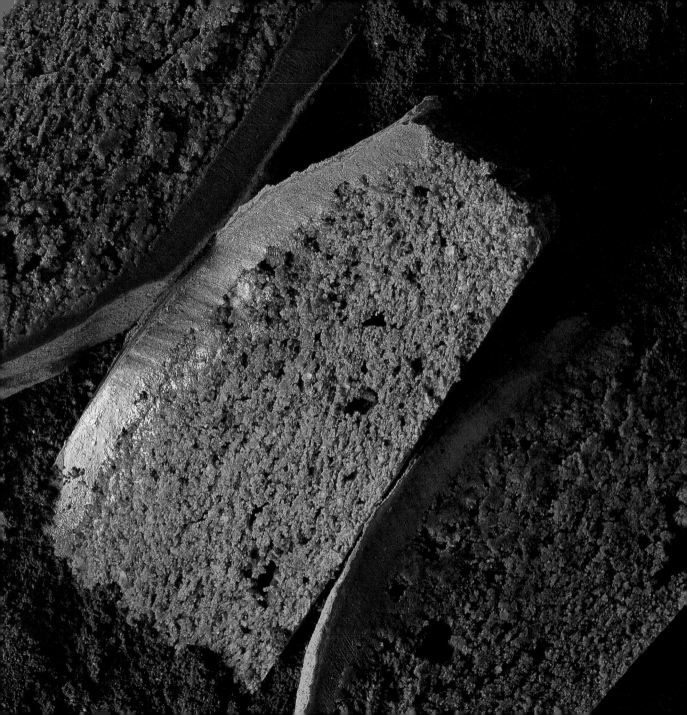

espresso cake

Sift the flour with the cocoa, salt, coffee and ground almonds.
In a mixing bowl, beat the butter until creamy using a wooden spoon or electric mixer.
Gradually beat in the sugar. When light and fluffy, beat in the eggs, 1 tablespoon at a time.
Carefully fold in the dry ingredients, hot water and alcohol.
Spoon into the prepared springform pan and smooth the surface. Bake in a preheated oven at 180°C (350°F) Gas 4 for about 40 minutes, or until a skewer inserted into the centre of the cake comes out clean. Carefully loosen the cake then unclip the pan. Let cool on a wire rack.
To make the icing, heat the cream until scalding hot, then remove from the heat and add the chocolate and coffee or alcohol. Leave until completely melted then stir gently. When cool and thick enough to spread, use to cover the top and sides of the cake. Leave until set, then store in an airtight container overnight before cutting.
Eat within 1 week, or freeze for up to 1 month.

*Finely **ground** espresso coffee rather than liquid coffee may seem a rather odd ingredient for this **moist** cake – but it tastes extraordinarily good!*

90 g cocoa powder

a pinch of salt

1 tablespoon very finely ground (espresso) coffee

120 g ground almonds

230 g unsalted butter

230 g golden caster sugar

225 g self-raising flour

4 large eggs, beaten

3 tablespoons very hot water

1 tablespoon coffee liqueur or brandy (optional)

Chocolate Icing:

150 ml double cream (not the extra-thick kind)

150 g plain dark chocolate, chopped

1 tablespoon very strong black coffee, coffee liqueur or brandy

one 24 cm springform pan, greased and base-lined

Makes 1 cake

Make this soft, moist, *flourless cake* with macadamias, pecans, walnuts, almonds or hazelnuts.
fudgy nut cake

350 g plain chocolate, chopped

175 g unsalted butter, diced

55 g cocoa powder, sifted

5 large eggs

1 teaspoon real vanilla essence

250 g golden caster sugar

100 g mixture of nuts,
roughly chopped

icing sugar and cocoa, for dusting

one 22 cm springform pan,
greased and base-lined

Makes 1 cake

Put the chopped chocolate and diced butter into a heatproof bowl set over a pan of steaming water. Stir frequently until melted and smooth. Remove from the heat, stir in the cocoa, then leave to cool.

Meanwhile in a large heatproof bowl, whisk the eggs, vanilla and sugar briefly until frothy. Set the bowl over a pan of steaming water – the water should not touch the base of the bowl. Using an electric hand whisk, whisk the mixture until it is very pale and thick – when the whisk is lifted it should leave a visible ribbon-like trail.

Remove the bowl from the heat, and whisk for a couple of minutes so the mixture cools. Using a large metal spoon, carefully fold in the chocolate mixture, followed by the nuts. When thoroughly combined, spoon into the prepared springform pan and smooth the surface.

Bake in a preheated oven at 180°C (350°F) Gas 4 for about 35 minutes or until firm to the touch but moist inside (do not overcook or the cake will be dry and hard to slice).

Let cool in the tin, then turn out and serve, dusted with cocoa and icing sugar. Store in an airtight container and eat within 1 week. It does not freeze well.

Rum-soaked **sultanas**, *butter, sugar, flour and cocoa – a* **terrific combination**. *Don't worry if the fruit sinks during baking.*

chocolate pound cake

70 g sultanas

3 tablespoons rum

4 large eggs, at room temperature

about 250 g unsalted butter, at room temperature

about 250 g golden caster sugar

50 g cocoa powder

about 200 g self-raising flour

a pinch of salt

one 900 g loaf tin, lined with a double thickness of greased greaseproof paper

Makes 1 large cake

Soak the sultanas in the rum, cover and set aside overnight. The next day, weigh the 4 eggs together and use exactly the same weight of butter and sugar.

To the 50 g of cocoa add enough of the flour to make the same weight. Sift the cocoa, flour and salt twice.

Put the measured soft butter in the bowl of an electric mixer and beat until creamy. Gradually beat in the measured sugar. After the last addition beat the mixture until it becomes very white and light in texture.

Beat the eggs in a separate bowl, then add to the butter mixture, 1 tablespoon at a time, beating well after each addition.

Using a large metal spoon, fold in the sifted flour mixture very gently. When thoroughly combined, fold in the sultanas and any rum left in the bowl.

Spoon into the prepared tin and smooth the surface. Bake in a preheated oven at 200°C (400°F) Gas 6 for 40–50 minutes or until a cocktail stick or skewer comes out clean.

Cool the cake in the tin for a couple of minutes, then lift it out and peel off the paper. Let cool completely on a wire rack. Store in an airtight container and eat within 1 week, or freeze up to 1 month.

devil's food cake

Gently melt the chopped chocolate, butter, sugar and syrup in a heavy pan over low heat, stirring frequently. Remove from the heat and let cool.

Sift the flour, cocoa and bicarbonate of soda into a mixing bowl and make a well in the centre. Pour in the melted mixture, stir gently, then add the eggs, vanilla and milk. Beat very gently with a wooden spoon until well mixed.

Spoon the mixture into the prepared tins and spread evenly. Bake in a preheated oven at 170°C (325°F) Gas 3 for about 15–20 minutes until just firm to the touch. Let cool before turning out of the tins.

To make the icing, heat the milk and sugar, stirring frequently until dissolved, then boil rapidly for 1 minute until syrupy. Remove from the heat and stir in the chopped chocolate. When melted and smooth, stir in the butter and vanilla. Let cool, stirring occasionally, then beat well until very thick. Spread one-third of this mixture on to one of the cakes and set the second on top. Spread the rest of the mixture evenly over the top and sides. Leave in a cool spot (not the fridge) until set. Store in an airtight container and eat within 5 days. The undecorated cakes can be frozen for up to 1 month.

An unusual, *quick* and *easy* method that produces a very dark cake – yet *light* and full of flavour.

90 g dark chocolate, chopped

115 g unsalted butter

90 g dark muscovado sugar

1 tablespoon golden syrup

175 g plain flour

25 g cocoa powder

½ teaspoon bicarbonate of soda

2 large eggs, beaten

½ teaspoon real vanilla essence

90 ml creamy milk

Chocolate Icing:

150 ml creamy milk

100 g golden caster sugar

60 g plain dark chocolate, chopped

60 g unsalted butter, at room temperature

½ teaspoon real vanilla essence

two 18 cm sandwich tins, greased and base-lined

Makes 1 cake

CHOCOLATE **BISCUITS**

chocolate crackles

115 g plain dark chocolate,
roughly chopped

115 g unsalted butter, diced,
at room temperature

1 large egg

2–3 drops real vanilla essence

175 g light brown
muscovado sugar

175 g self-raising flour

½ teaspoon bicarbonate of soda

about 2 tablespoons icing sugar,
for coating

several baking sheets, greased

Makes about 28

Melt the chopped chocolate gently in a heatproof bowl set over a pan of barely simmering water, stirring frequently. Remove the bowl from the heat and gradually stir in the butter. In another bowl, whisk the egg and vanilla until frothy using a wire whisk or electric mixer. Gradually whisk in the sugar, followed by the chocolate mixture.

Sift the flour and bicarbonate of soda into the bowl, then stir in to make a firm dough. In hot weather or if the dough seems sticky, wrap it and chill for 15 minutes.

Using your hands, roll the dough into walnut-sized balls. Roll each ball in icing sugar, then arrange, spaced well apart, on the prepared baking sheets.

Bake in a preheated oven at 200°C (400°F) Gas 6 for about 10–12 minutes until just firm.

Cool for 1 minute until firm enough to transfer to a wire rack to cool completely.

Store in an airtight container and eat within 1 week, or freeze for up to 1 month.

*These biscuits **crack** and spread in the oven — finish with a dusting of icing sugar to make them look even more **dramatic**.*

*Cut these shortbread biscuits into any **pretty** shape, then bake, cool and dip in chocolate.*

cinnamon
chocolate stars

Using a wooden spoon or electric mixer beat the butter until creamy. Gradually beat in the sugar. When the mixture is pale and fluffy, sift the flour, salt, cinnamon and rice flour into the bowl and mix. When the mixture comes together, turn it on to a lightly floured surface and knead lightly and briefly to make a smooth, but not sticky dough. In hot weather, or if the dough feels sticky, wrap it and chill until firm. Roll out the dough about 5 mm thick and cut out shapes with the cutter. Gently knead together the trimmings, then re-roll and cut more stars.

Arrange the stars slightly apart on the prepared baking sheets. Prick with a fork and chill for about 15 minutes. Bake the biscuits in a preheated oven at 180°C (350°F) Gas 4 for 12–15 minutes or until firm and barely coloured. Let cool on the baking sheets for a couple of minutes until firm enough to transfer to a wire cooling rack. When completely cold, gently melt the chocolate in a small heatproof bowl set over a pan of steaming water. Stir until smooth, then remove the bowl from the heat. Dip the points of the stars in to the melted chocolate, then leave to set on waxed paper, non-stick parchment or a wire rack. When firm, store in an airtight container and eat within 3 days. Undecorated biscuits can be frozen for up to 1 month.

180 g unsalted butter, at room temperature

90 g golden caster sugar

230 g plain flour

a good pinch of salt

1 teaspoon ground cinnamon

40 g rice flour, ground rice or cornflour

50 g plain dark chocolate, to finish

one medium star-shaped cutter

several baking sheets, greased

Makes about 30

black and white
biscuits

115 g unsalted butter,
at room temperature

85 g light brown muscovado sugar

1 large egg, beaten

60 g self-raising flour

½ teaspoon baking powder

a pinch of salt

½ teaspoon real vanilla essence

115 g porridge oats

175 g plain dark chocolate,
chopped into chunks

several baking sheets, greased

Makes about 24

Beat the butter until creamy using a wooden spoon or electric mixer. Add the sugar and beat until light and creamy. Gradually beat in the egg, and beat well after the last addition. Sift the flour with the baking powder and salt into the mixing bowl, add the vanilla essence and oats, and stir in. When thoroughly combined, stir in the chocolate chunks. Put heaped teaspoons of the mixture, spaced well apart, on the prepared sheets, then bake in a preheated oven at 180°C (350°F) Gas 4 for 12–15 minutes until golden and just firm. Let cool on the sheets for a couple of minutes until firm enough to transfer to a wire rack.

Let cool completely, then store in an airtight container. Eat within 1 week or freeze for up to 1 month.

*Make chocolate chips by chopping good **dark** chocolate into large chunks – the flavour is far **superior** to the commercial chocolate chips.*

Chocolate **chip** *biscuits with a difference – the dough is flavoured with melted chocolate plus* **chunks** *of plain chocolate.*

giant double chocolate nut biscuits

140 g plain chocolate, chopped

100 g unsalted butter,
at room temperature

80 g golden caster sugar

80 g dark brown muscovado sugar

1 large egg, beaten

½ teaspoon real vanilla essence

150 g plain flour

a pinch of salt

½ teaspoon baking powder

50 g pecans or walnuts, chopped

100 g plain dark (or white)
chocolate, chopped into chunks

several baking sheets, greased

Makes 16

In a heatproof bowl, gently melt the 140 g chopped chocolate over a pan of barely simmering water. Remove from the heat and let cool.

Meanwhile beat the butter until creamy using a wooden spoon or electric mixer. Add the sugars and beat again until light and fluffy. Gradually beat in the egg and vanilla essence, followed by the melted chocolate.

Sift the flour into the bowl with the salt and baking powder and stir. When thoroughly combined, work in the chopped nuts and chocolate chunks.

Put heaped tablespoons of dough, spaced well apart, on to the prepared baking sheets.

Bake in a preheated oven at 180°C (350°F) Gas 4 for about 12–15 minutes until just firm. Cool for a couple of minutes until firm enough to transfer to a wire rack to cool completely. Store in an airtight container. Eat within 1 week or freeze for up to 1 month.

squillionaire's
shortbread

397 g canned condensed milk,
for the filling

120 g unsalted butter,
at room temperature

60 g golden caster sugar

160 g plain flour

20 g cocoa powder

Chocolate Topping:

160 g plain dark chocolate
chopped

30 g unsalted butter, diced

about 50 g white chocolate,
to finish

one 20 cm square cake tin,
5 cm deep, greased

Makes 16

Put the unopened can of condensed milk in a heavy pan and
cover with water. Bring to the boil, then simmer without
covering the pan for 3½ hours. Top up the water regularly: the
can must always be covered. Cool the can completely before
opening. The condensed milk should have become a fudgy,
dark, golden caramel.

Meanwhile, to make the chocolate biscuit base, beat the
butter until creamy, then beat in the sugar. When the mixture
is light and fluffy, sift the flour with the cocoa into the bowl
and work with your hands to make a smooth dough. Press the
dough into the prepared cake tin to make an even layer. Prick
well with a fork and chill for 15 minutes.

Bake the biscuit base in a preheated oven at 180°C (350°F)
Gas 4 for 20 minutes until just firm and very slightly darker
around the edges – do not overcook or it will taste bitter.
Let cool in the tin. When completely cold, spread the cold
caramel over the top. Chill until firm – about 1–2 hours.

To make the topping, melt the chopped dark chocolate in a
heatproof bowl set over a pan of barely simmering water.
Remove from the heat and stir in the butter. When smooth,
spread over the caramel, then leave to set. Melt the white
chocolate in the same way, then drizzle over the top of the
dark chocolate using a fork or a greaseproof paper icing bag.
Leave overnight until firm before cutting. Store in an airtight
container and eat within 1 week. Not suitable for freezing.

three-chocolate
squares

Melt the dark chocolate gently in a heatproof bowl set over a pan of barely simmering water. Stir occasionally. Remove the bowl from the heat and let cool.

Meanwhile beat the butter until creamy with a wooden spoon or electric mixer. Add the sugar and vanilla and beat well. Gradually beat in the egg, followed by the cooled chocolate. Sift the flour with the baking powder, bicarbonate of soda and cocoa powder into another bowl. Using a metal spoon, fold the flour mixture into the chocolate mixture in 3 batches alternating with the soured cream.

When thoroughly combined, spoon into the prepared tin and smooth the surface.

Bake in a preheated oven at 190°C (375°F) Gas 5 until just firm – 25–30 minutes. Let cool in the tin before turning out. To make the topping, melt the white chocolate as before, then stir in the butter. When smooth, spread over the cake and leave until set.

Cut into 16 pieces and store in an airtight container. Eat within 5 days or freeze for up to 1 month.

Three kinds of chocolate – white, plain and cocoa – make great little cakes, good with coffee.

**60 g plain dark chocolate,
chopped**

**120 g unsalted butter,
at room temperature**

**170 g light brown
muscovado sugar**

½ teaspoon real vanilla essence

1 large egg, beaten

220 g plain flour

1 teaspoon baking powder

½ teaspoon bicarbonate of soda

25 g cocoa powder

150 ml soured cream

White Chocolate Topping:

**50 g good quality white
chocolate, chopped**

**20 g unsalted butter,
at room temperature**

one 20 cm square cake tin,
greased and base-lined

Makes 16

fudge brownies

140 g unsalted butter

4 large eggs, beaten

340 g light brown
muscovado sugar

1 teaspoon real vanilla essence

a good pinch of salt

75 g cocoa powder

140 g plain flour

100 g walnut or pecan pieces,
chopped white or plain chocolate,
or a combination

one 23 cm square cake tin, 5 cm
deep, completely lined with foil

Makes 16

Gently melt the butter in a pan and let cool while preparing
the rest of the mixture.

Using a wooden spoon, beat the eggs very gently with the
sugar until just blended and free of lumps. Stir in the cooled
butter and the vanilla. Sift the salt, cocoa and flour together
into the bowl and gently stir in – do not beat or overmix, or
the brownies will become cake-like.

When combined, fold in the nuts or chocolate. Pour into the
prepared tin and smooth the surface.

Bake in a preheated oven at 170°C (325°F) Gas 3 for about
35–40 minutes or until a skewer inserted midway between the
centre and the side of the tin comes out clean. The centre
should be just firm – do not overcook or they will be dry.

Put the tin on a damp tea towel to cool completely.

Lift the brownies out of the tin still in the foil, remove the foil
and cut into 16 squares.

Store in an airtight container and eat within 1 week or freeze
for up to 1 month.

A wonderful version of one of the great **American** classics.

blondies

140 g unsalted butter

400 g light brown
muscovado sugar

1 teaspoon real vanilla essence

3 large eggs, beaten

300 g plain flour

1 teaspoon baking powder

a large pinch of salt

50 g walnut pieces,
roughly chopped

50 g good white chocolate,
roughly chopped

50 g plain dark chocolate,
roughly chopped

one 30 x 22 cm roasting
or baking tin, lined with foil

Makes 48

Put the butter into a large, heavy pan and melt gently. Add the sugar, stir well, then remove from the heat. Cool for 1 minute, then stir in the vanilla essence and the eggs.

Sift the flour, baking powder and salt into the pan and stir just until thoroughly blended – do not beat or overmix.

Pour the mixture into the prepared tin and spread evenly.

Sprinkle the nuts and chopped chocolate over the top.

Bake in a preheated oven at 180°C (350°F) Gas 4 for about 25 minutes until just firm.

Cool for a few minutes in the tin then lift the cake, still in the foil, on to a wire rack to cool completely.

Remove the foil and cut into 48 squares. Store in an airtight container and eat within 4 days. They can be frozen for up to 1 month, but they will be stickier than freshly baked ones.

*Pale-gold brownies, **topped** with **nuts** and **two** kinds of chocolate – dark and white.*

A *delicate* mixture flavoured with finely ground coffee.
mocha madeleines

Melt the butter and chocolate gently in a heatproof bowl set over a pan of barely simmering water, stirring frequently. Remove from the heat and let cool.

Meanwhile, sift the flour twice with the cocoa, salt and coffee, then set aside. Using an electric mixer, whisk the eggs with the sugar until the mixture becomes pale and thick – when the whisk is lifted out the mixture should leave a ribbon-like trail on the surface. Using a large metal spoon, fold the flour mixture into the egg mixture in 3 batches, then carefully fold in the chocolate mixture until all are thoroughly combined (the mixture will lose a little bulk).

Put a heaped teaspoon or so of the mixture into each madeleine mould so it is two-thirds full.

Bake in a preheated oven at 190°C (375°F) Gas 5 for about 10–12 minutes or until just firm.

Let cool for 1 minute, then remove from the moulds using a round-bladed knife.

Cool on a wire rack, then dust with icing sugar.

Store in an airtight container and eat within 1 week or freeze for up to 1 month.

140 g unsalted butter, diced

85 g dark chocolate, chopped

140 g plain flour

2 tablespoons good cocoa powder

a pinch of salt

1 teaspoon finely ground espresso coffee

4 large eggs

140 g golden caster sugar

icing sugar, for dusting

madeleine moulds, twice buttered*

Makes 30

*Non-stick moulds work best. If using ordinary metal moulds, brush with 2 coats of melted butter, and chill between applications.

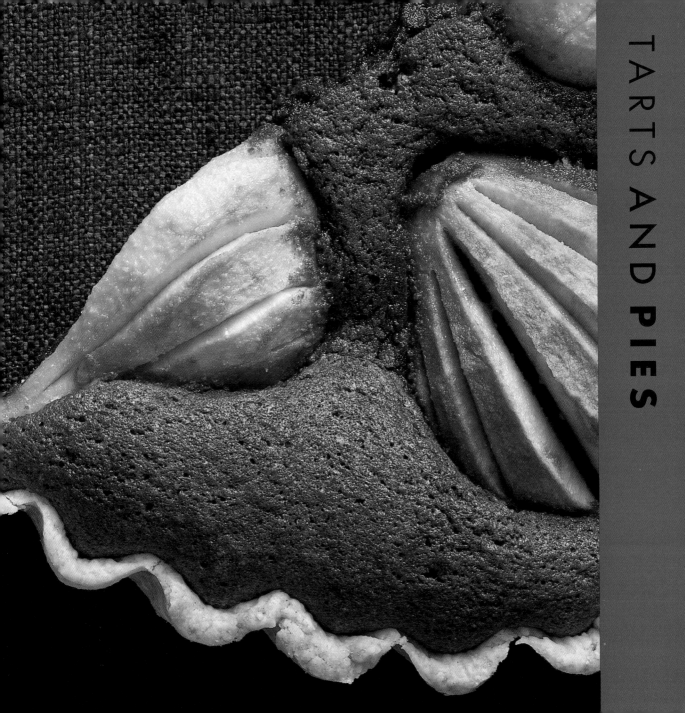

TARTS AND **PIES**

chocolate pear tart

180 g plain flour

110 g unsalted butter,
chilled and diced

35 g golden caster sugar

1 egg yolk

about 1 tablespoon iced water

Chocolate Pear Filling:

125 g dark chocolate, chopped

125 g unsalted butter,
at room temperature

90 g golden caster sugar

4 large eggs, separated

125 g ground almonds

2–3 drops real almond essence

a pinch of salt

2 ripe medium-sized pears

one 23 cm deep loose-based
flan tin

a baking tray

Makes 1 tart, serves 8

To make the pastry, sift the flour into a bowl, and rub in the diced butter with the tips of your fingers until the mixture resembles fine crumbs.

Stir in the sugar, add the egg yolk and water, then bind the mixture together using a pastry-blender or round-bladed knife, such as a table knife. If the dough is dry and crumbly, add a little extra water.

Without kneading, quickly bring the dough together with your hands to make a soft but not sticky ball.

To make the dough in a food processor, put the flour, butter and sugar into the bowl and process until the mixture resembles fine crumbs. With the machine running, add the yolk and water through the feed tube and process just until the dough comes together.

Wrap and chill the dough for 20 minutes. On a lightly floured surface, roll out the pastry to a circle about 29 cm across. Line the flan tin with it. Chill while preparing the filling.

Put a baking tray into a preheated oven 200°C (400°F) Gas 6 to heat up – this helps to make the pastry base crisp.

To make the filling, very gently melt the chocolate in a heatproof bowl set over a pan of barely simmering water. Stir until smooth, then remove from the heat and let cool. Meanwhile, using an electric mixer or wooden spoon, beat the butter until creamy, then beat in the sugar. When the mixture is light and fluffy, beat in the egg yolks one at a time, beating well after each addition. Beat in the cooled chocolate, then stir in the almonds and essence using a large metal spoon.

In a spotlessly clean greasefree bowl, whisk the egg whites with the pinch of salt until they form soft peaks. Using a large metal spoon, gently fold them into the chocolate mixture in 3 batches. Spoon into the prepared chilled pastry case and spread evenly.

Peel and halve the pears, then scoop out the cores with a melon-baller or pointed teaspoon. Thinly slice the pear halves, leaving the slices attached at the stalk end, so they resemble fans. Arrange the pears on top of the chocolate mixture in a neat pattern.

Set the flan tin on the heated baking tray and bake for 15 minutes, then reduce the oven temperature to 180°C (350°F) Gas 4 and bake for about 10 minutes longer or until the tart is just cooked in the centre – test by piercing the filling with a skewer.

Very carefully unmould and serve either warm or at room temperature with crème fraîche or vanilla ice cream. The tart tastes better the day after baking, though it sinks slightly.

Variation:

Chocolate Normandy Tart

Substitute crisp, tart eating apples for the pears and prepare them in the same way. Add ½ teaspoon ground cinnamon to the chocolate filling, and proceed as in the main recipe.

Use just-ripe **Comice** pears for this **rich**, not-too-sweet tart.

Serve warm, at room temperature, or **chilled** *with vanilla ice cream, crème fraîche or chocolate sauce.*

chestnut and chocolate
moneybags

about 300 g filo pastry

250 g curd cheese

40 g dark muscovado sugar

2 medium egg yolks

2–3 tablespoons rum

200 g plain dark chocolate, coarsely grated

120 g drained cooked chestnuts, roughly chopped (vacuum packed or canned in light syrup or water)

60 g unsalted butter, melted, for brushing

icing sugar for dusting

several baking trays

Makes 12, serves 4–6

If necessary defrost the pastry according to the packet instructions. (Filo varies enormously between brands. Some are very good: others turn out tough and leathery.)

To make the filling, beat the curd cheese until softened using a wooden spoon, then beat in the sugar followed by the egg yolks. Add rum to taste. Using a metal spoon, gently stir in the grated chocolate and the chestnuts.

Remove the pastry from the box and cover with a damp tea towel until ready to use – the sheets of dough dry out very easily and become unusable.

Put 3 sheets on a work surface and cut into 18 cm squares. Put a good tablespoon of the mixture ($\frac{1}{12}$ of the amount) into the centre of each square, gather up the edges and twist the top to resemble a pastry money bag. There is no need to dampen the edges of the pastry. Repeat to make 12. Arrange, spaced well apart on the baking trays and chill for about 15 minutes.

Brush with melted butter, then bake in a preheated oven at 190°C (375°F) Gas 5 for about 15 minutes until golden brown. Serve, dusted with icing sugar.

southern deep-dish
pecan pie

180 g plain flour

a pinch of salt

110 g unsalted butter,
chilled and diced

35 g caster sugar

1 egg yolk

about 1 tablespoon
iced water, to bind

Pecan Filling:

220 g light brown
muscovado sugar

300 ml double cream

70 g plain dark chocolate,
chopped

2 medium egg yolks

½ teaspoon real vanilla essence

1 tablespoon bourbon (optional)

150 g pecan halves

shaved or grated white chocolate
'curls', to finish

one 23 cm loose-based
deep flan tin

Makes 1 pie, serves 8–10

If using a food processor, put the flour and salt into the bowl. Add the butter and process until fine crumbs are formed. Add the sugar and process briefly. With the machine running, add the egg yolk and water and process until the dough comes together. Wrap and chill for 20 minutes until firm.

Roll out the dough to a large circle about 29 cm across and use to line the flan tin. Prick well and chill for 15 minutes. To bake the pastry blind, fill with a round of baking parchment and baking beans and cook in a preheated oven at 200°C (400°F) Gas 6 for about 15 minutes until firm. Remove the paper and beans and return the pastry case, still in its tin, to the oven for 5–10 minutes until crisp and golden. Let cool. To prepare the filling, put the sugar and cream into a heavy pan and stir over medium heat until the sugar has melted and the mixture is almost boiling. Remove from the heat and stir in the chocolate. When smooth add the egg yolks and mix well. Stir over very low heat until the mixture thickens. Remove from the heat and stir in the vanilla, bourbon (if using) and nuts. Pour into the prepared pastry case and chill until firm. Serve decorated with white chocolate curls – these are made using a vegetable peeler or grater.

Eat within 3 days. Not suitable for freezing.

A pecan pie *with nuts, chocolate* and American *bourbon*.

amaretti chocolate
cheesecake

To make the crust, mix the butter and amaretti crumbs then press on to the base of the prepared tin in an even layer. Chill while making the filling.

To make the filling, chop the chocolate and melt it gently in a heatproof bowl set over a pan of steaming water. Remove from the heat, stir until smooth, then let cool.

Put the cream cheese, eggs and sugar into the bowl of a food processor and process until thoroughly combined. Add the cream and process again until just mixed. With the machine running add the melted chocolate and Amaretto, if using, through the feed tube, and process until smooth.

Spoon the filling into the prepared tin and smooth the surface. Bake in a preheated oven at 170°C (325°F) Gas 3 for 40 minutes until firm. Let cool in the oven with the door ajar. When completely cold, chill overnight.

Unclip the tin and remove the cheesecake. Decorate the top with the broken amaretti biscuits. Drizzle with melted chocolate, using either a greaseproof paper icing bag with the end snipped off, or a fork dipped in the chocolate.

Store the cheesecake in a covered container in the fridge then remove 30 minutes before serving. Eat within 5 days or freeze for up to 1 month.

*Amaretti add **crunchy** texture and nutty taste to this easy recipe.*

60 g unsalted butter, melted

100 g amaretti biscuits, crushed

Chocolate Filling:

200 g plain dark chocolate

400 g Philadelphia cream cheese

2 medium eggs

60 g caster sugar

200 ml double cream

50 ml Amaretto liqueur (optional)

To Finish:

6 amaretti biscuits, broken

40 g plain dark chocolate, melted

one 21 cm springform tin, greased

Serves 12

*A **thoroughly** self-indulgent, grown-up **version** of a traditional nursery pudding.*

chocolate rice pudding

30 g plain chocolate, chopped

550 ml creamy milk

35 g round-grained rice

25 g golden caster sugar

1 vanilla pod*

one 750 ml ovenproof baking dish, very well buttered

Serves 4

The vanilla pod can be rinsed carefully, dried, then used again.

Heat the chocolate and milk gently in a pan just until melted, stirring occasionally. Let cool. Put the rice, sugar and vanilla pod in the buttered dish and pour in the chocolate milk. Stir gently, then bake in a preheated oven at 150°C (300°F) Gas 2 for about 2½ hours until the rice is tender and the pudding thickened. Serve warm.

Variation:

Chocolate Rice Cream

This variation is cooked on top of the stove. Omit the vanilla and put the remaining ingredients in a saucepan with 3 green cardamom pods. Bring to the boil, stirring, then simmer for 40 minutes until the rice is soft. Remove the cardamom. Stir in 1 egg yolk and cook 1 minute. Pour into a serving dish or dishes, cool, cover and chill. Serve icy cold, sprinkled with icing sugar or a drizzle of cream.

hot white
chocolate pudding

Melt the chopped chocolate in a heatproof bowl set over a pan of barely simmering water. Remove from the heat and stir until smooth.

Using a wooden spoon or electric mixer, beat the butter until creamy, then gradually beat in the sugar. When the mixture is very light and fluffy, beat in the eggs, 1 tablespoon at a time, beating well after each addition.

Using a metal spoon, carefully fold in the flour and salt, then fold in the melted chocolate, vanilla essence and enough milk to give a soft, dropping consistency.

Spoon into the prepared dish – it should be two-thirds full. Cover loosely with buttered foil and bake in a preheated oven at 180°C (350°F) Gas 4 for about 35 minutes or until firm. Meanwhile, to make the chocolate custard, heat the milk in a saucepan until scalding hot. Sift the cocoa, sugar and cornflour into a bowl and mix to a thick paste with the egg yolks and about 1 tablespoon of the milk.

Stir in the remaining milk, then return the mixture to the pan. Stir over low heat until very hot, thickened and smooth – do not allow to boil. Serve immediately with the pudding.

80 g white chocolate, chopped

115 g unsalted butter,
at room temperature

115 g golden caster sugar

2 large eggs, beaten

150 g self-raising flour

a pinch of salt

a few drops real vanilla essence

about 3 tablespoons milk

Chocolate Custard:

425 ml creamy milk

20 g cocoa powder

55 g golden caster sugar

15 g cornflour

2 medium egg yolks

one 750 ml baking dish, well greased

Serves 4

*A cold weather **treat** – baked chocolate **sponge** pudding, served with chocolate **custard**.*

A wonderfully rich, light, smooth soufflé with a surprise filling.
rich chocolate soufflé

Brush melted butter inside the ramekins and sprinkle with caster sugar. Stand on a baking sheet or in a roasting tin. Put the chocolate and cream into a heavy-based pan. Set over very low heat and stir occasionally until melted. Remove from the heat and stir gently until smooth. Gently stir in the egg yolks, one at a time, then half the brandy or liqueur. Put the 5 egg whites into a spotlessly clean, grease-free bowl and whisk until stiff peaks form. Sprinkle with the sugar and briefly whisk again to make a smooth, stiff meringue. If you over-whisk the meringue at this stage it will do more harm than good, and the end result will be less smooth. The chocolate mixture should be just warm, so gently reheat it if necessary. Using a large metal spoon, mix in a little of the meringue to loosen the consistency. Pour the chocolate mixture on top of the meringue and gently fold together until thoroughly combined but not over-mixed. Half-fill the prepared ramekins. Spoon the remaining brandy or liqueur over the amaretti biscuits then put one in the centre of each ramekin. Add the remaining mixture until the ramekins are full almost to the rim.

Bake in a preheated oven at 220°C (425°F) Gas 7 for 8–10 minutes. Remove from the oven when they are barely set (the centres should be soft and wobble when gently shaken). Sprinkle with icing sugar and serve immediately.

170 g plain chocolate, broken into small squares

140 ml double cream

3 medium eggs, separated, plus 2 egg whites

4 tablespoons brandy or Amaretto liqueur

3 tablespoons caster sugar

4 amaretti biscuits

icing sugar, for sprinkling

four 300 ml ovenproof ramekin dishes, buttered and sugared

Serves 4

A velvety *smooth* finale for a *special* dinner party – serve this terrine with very strong coffee.

chocolate terrine

400 g plain dark chocolate, roughly chopped

40 g cocoa powder

3 tablespoons strong espresso coffee

2 tablespoons brandy

6 large eggs, at room temperature

100 g golden caster sugar

250 ml double cream, chilled

one loaf tin, 22 x 11 x 7 cm deep, greased and base-lined

one bain-marie or roasting tin

Serves 8

Put the chopped chocolate into a heatproof bowl with the cocoa and coffee. Set over a pan of barely simmering water and melt gently, stirring frequently. Remove the bowl from the heat, stir in the brandy and let cool.

Meanwhile put the eggs into the bowl of an electric mixer and whisk until frothy. Add the sugar and whisk until the mixture is pale and very thick – the whisk should leave a ribbon-like trail when lifted.

In another bowl, whip the cream until it holds a soft peak. Using a large metal spoon, gently fold the chocolate mixture into the eggs. When combined, fold in the whipped cream. Spoon the mixture into the prepared tin, then stand the tin in a bain-marie (a roasting tin half-filled with warm water). Bake in a preheated oven at 170°C (325°F) Gas 3 for about 1–1¼ hours or until a skewer inserted into the centre of the mixture comes out clean.

Remove from the oven, let cool in the bain-marie for about 45 minutes, then lift the tin out of the bain-marie and leave until completely cold.

Chill overnight then turn out. Serve dusted with icing sugar. Store, well wrapped in the refrigerator, for up to 5 days.

This pudding is very **rich**, *so serve in* **small** *portions.*

chocolate brûlée

600 ml thick single cream or thin pouring double cream (avoid extra-thick double cream)

1 vanilla pod, split

300 g plain dark chocolate, finely chopped

4 medium egg yolks

60 g icing sugar, sifted

about 3 tablespoons caster sugar, for sprinkling

eight 150 ml ramekins

one bain-marie or roasting tin

Serves 8

In a heavy pan, heat the cream with the split vanilla pod until scalding hot but not boiling. Remove from the heat, cover and leave to infuse for 15 minutes.

Lift out the vanilla pod and scrape the seeds into the cream with the tip of a small knife.

Stir the chocolate into the cream until melted and smooth.

Put the egg yolks and icing sugar into a medium sized bowl, beat with a wooden spoon until well blended, then stir in the warm chocolate cream. When thoroughly combined, pour into the ramekin dishes.

Stand the dishes in a bain-marie (a roasting tin half-filled with warm water) and bake in a preheated oven at 180°C (350°F) Gas 4 for about 30 minutes until just firm. Remove from the bain-marie and let cool. Cover and chill overnight or for up to 48 hours.

Sprinkle a little sugar over the tops, then put under a very hot grill for just a few minutes to caramelize. A warning: if the ramekins are left for too long under the grill the chocolate cream will melt. Serve within 1 hour.